Riding in Gem Park

by Antonio Colantoni
illustrated by Ellen Joy Sasaki

Core Decodable 66

McGraw Hill Education

Bothell, WA • Chicago, IL • Columbus, OH • New York, NY

MHEonline.com

Send all inquiries to:
McGraw-Hill Education
8787 Orion Place
Columbus, OH 43240

ISBN: 978-0-02-144345-1
MHID: 0-02-144345-9

Printed in the United States of America.

7 8 9 LCR 25 24 23

Gem Park is a large park.
It has a nice bike path.

The path is flat at first.
And it is cement.

The cement path lasts a mile.
It runs past Pine River.

After the bridge, the path changes.
It is not as flat.

The path is uphill.
And it is gravel and cinders.

The hill is gentle at first.
The ride is not bad.

Then the ride is hard.
Tires slip on the cinders.

If riders get tired, they rest.
They do not have to race.

The path is on a giant cliff.
A fence makes it safe.

At the hilltop, it's quiet.
You see much in the distance.

At the top, the path turns.
It starts down the hill.

Riders check bike brakes.
They will glide down fast.

The path twists and turns.
It passes the concert shell.

The path ends at the giant rock.
What a fun and wild ride!